ALASKA

This edition published in 1987
by SMITHMARK Publishers Inc.,
112 Madison Avenue
New York, New York 10016

SMITHMARK books are available for bulk purchase for sales
promotion and premium use. For details write or telephone the
Manager of Special Sales, SMITHMARK Publishers Inc., 112
Madison Avenue, New York, NY 10016. (212) 532-6600.

Produced by Brompton Books Corp.,
15 Sherwood Place
Greenwich, CT 06830

ISBN 0-8317-0212-5

Printed in Hong Kong

10 9 8 7 6 5 4 3 2 1

AND THE YUKON

TEXT   JOYCE WALKER

DESIGN   MIKE ROSE

SMITHMARK

Dedication

To my travelling companion and sister,
Betsy Paulding Kelley.

*3-6 A panoramic view in Alaska's Denali National
Park of Mount McKinley and the Thorofare River
at sunset.*

INTRODUCTION

The vast wilderness of Alaska and the Yukon, in the extreme northwest of North America, unite Canada and the United States in a shared landscape of sharp-ridged mountain ranges and rolling tundra, crystal clear winding rivers and deep green lakes. Comprising one of the world's last frontiers — but a frontier to be explored, not conquered — Alaska and the Yukon represent a primitive ideal. The challenges of this rugged land come to define the character of those who inhabit it. Captured and popularized in the writings of Jack London, Robert W Service and John Muir, Alaska and the Yukon are rich in history and diversity. Thousands of images crowd the memory of anyone who has lived or visited here: steep mountains rising sharply from the sea, evergreens etched in frost under a moonlit sky, the purple light of the midnight sun glimmering on the Arctic Ocean, the genuine smile on an Eskimo face from deep within a fur-trimmed hood, the festive sight of the red barns and bright green grass of the Matanuska Valley, the glow of cabin lights across the snow on a winter night, a moose cow and her calf pausing to drink at the Yukon's beautiful Kluane Lake.

At least 25,000 years ago, Mongolian people made their way onto what is now North America via the Bering land bridge. Hunters probably following game, they migrated steadily until the melting glaciers gradually submerged the land bridge. Some of these early nomads would wander south; others would stay to establish themselves as the ancestors of contemporary natives of Alaska and the Yukon. Abundant game yielded easy subsistence to these adventurers. Its proximity making Russian contact inevitable. Alaska was first explored by Russians in the early eighteenth century. Hired by the Russian Tsar, Peter the Great, to explore eastern waters, the Danish Captain Vitus

Bering discovered the Alaska mainland in 1741, after working his way up the Aleutian Chain. The land would be further explored, as some place names testify, by the Spanish, British and French, but the Russians claimed and colonized 'Russian America' (named Alaska after the Aleut word for 'the great land'). Centered first on Kodiak Island and later in the more sheltered Sitka of the southeastern Panhandle, Russian culture adapted to its hardy new environs. Trade flourished in many directions, ships for example transporting ice south for San Francisco's many taverns, and returning with food. But the greatest demand was for fur, especially in Europe and Asia, and the fur seal was hunted at its breeding ground in the Pribilof Islands practically to extinction.

Imperial Russia was finding its eastern colony expensive to maintain, and in 1867 US Secretary of State William Seward negotiated for the purchase of the vast property. At two and a half cents an acre, the $7.2 million purchase was promptly dubbed 'Seward's Icebox,' at least until the discovery of gold there in 1880. A series of subsequent gold strikes across the land, which became a territory in 1912, brought Alaska into the public eye. Goldseekers endured any hardship to give themselves a chance at the thousands of dollars they dreamed lay waiting to be harvested. Most would of course be disappointed, and most would leave, but a particular kind of person would be drawn to this strange new land, staying on as suppliers to the goldseekers, as trappers and as guides.

About the same time as the gold boom in Alaska, George Washington Carmacks, Skookum Jim and Tagish Charlie were making themselves part of Yukon history. Their discovery of gold there in the summer of 1896 touched off the creation of the Yukon Territory, then a part of the District of Mackenzie. The bonechilling ascent up Chilkoot Pass in the days of the great Klondike Gold Rush was the stuff of legend — and of heartbreak. Columns many miles long of goldseekers trudged through the snow into the Yukon's interior, after reaching the end of the line by boat. Thousands arrived at Dawson City, the gateway to the gold fields, to find all the claims staked and little to do, after their arduous journey, but wander the streets in a daze of disbelief. Many had sold all their belongings and given up their lives elsewhere in pursuit of this incredible dream. As in Alaska, most would eventually leave, but others would discover a different kind of riches the Yukon had to offer.

The territories of the Yukon and Alaska were slow to develop. In 1935 farmers from the United States' drought-stricken Midwest emigrated to Alaska's fertile Matanuska Valley, northeast of Anchorage. The summer's long days are responsible for some of the largest and most abundant crops in the country, as witnessed at Alaska's annual State Fair in Palmer, where 7-pound turnips and 70-pound cabbages amaze onlookers! Stirred by a sudden recognition of Alaska's strategic position and the need for national defense, the US government created military installations in Alaska during World War II. At the same time the building of the Alaska Highway was begun, a 1520-mile highway which unites many parts of the Yukon and Alaska.

In Alaska a different kind of gold brought new popularity and investment to the territory, which became the forty-ninth state in 1959. Oil discoveries on the North Slope eventually gave rise to one of the largest of such projects in the history of the country: the trans-Alaska pipeline. Completed in 1977, the pipeline carries one and a half million barrels of oil a day from Prudhoe

Bay on the Arctic Ocean to its southern terminus at Valdez on the Gulf of Alaska. Before Alaska's oil resources could be exploited, however, both environmental and native land claim concerns had to be satisfied. In 1971 the Native Lands Claim Settlement Act allocated $900 million and 44 million acres in compensation to Alaska's native people, to be administered by Native Regional Corporations comprised of Indians, Eskimos and Aleuts. The 1964 earthquake that hit Anchorage, and the 1967 floods that devastated Fairbanks brought further national attention and concern to Alaska. Today America's largest and most northwestern state has a population of 500,000, a figure which is steadily increasing.

Encompassing 586,400 square miles, Alaska is almost nine times larger than New England and more than twice the size of Texas. With 5000 glaciers and about three million freshwater lakes, Alaska's landscape offers much for the naturalist to explore. Meandering rivers sculpt valleys through forest and hillside. The so-called Panhandle region of Alaska, a narrow strip of land and archipelego that dips to the southeast, features lush forested islands separated from the mainland by the famed Inside Passage. Marine ferries provide transportation between the many islands, and some of the world's best fishing is found here. The climate is mild and moist. Glacier Bay National Park and Preserve in the Panhandle's northern stem sprawls across the St Elias Mountains. Tidewater glaciers make their way from sharply-rising snow-capped mountains, filling deep fjords with the bluish forms of icebergs.

The huge peninsula that forms most of Alaska, dotted with cities such as international Anchorage and modern Fairbanks, remains largely wilderness, with only one-fifth of the state accessible by road. Alaska's topography is shaped by the Pacific and Arctic mountain systems, a central plateau and the Arctic slope.

Sharing highways, rivers and mountain ranges, Alaska and the Yukon are political divisions of a contiguous geography. The Yukon's 186,600 square miles stretch from the Beaufort Sea south to British Columbia, and from its western boundary with Alaska to the vast Northwest Territories. Untamed and exhilarating, the Yukon supports only 23,000 people, more than half of whom live in or near the capital of Whitehorse. The days of the Klondike are re-enacted in Dawson City, which celebrates Discovery Day with a raft race on the Klondike River. Diamond Tooth Gertie's features gaming tables and can-can girls, while outlying ghost towns and played-out lodes give their own testimony to a dramatic chapter in Yukon history.

The lure of living close to nature still beckons in Alaska and the Yukon. A tradition of rugged individualism combined with unabashed friendliness lends dimension to a place that is much more than its wilderness landscape. The hospitable chatter of a bush pilot, the sight of a fishing boat returning with an escort of excited seagulls, a kayak skimming over a placid lake, the muted colors of a seemingly-endless tundra, the setting sun reflected in the mighty Yukon River — these are the impressions that recall the vast and untamed land that is Alaska and the Yukon.

COASTLINE AND ISLANDS

With more shoreline than any other state, Alaska has a wealth of resources in its fishing and marine transportation industries. From the Alexander Archipelego of the southeastern Panhandle region, composed of about 1000 islands scattered off a thin strip of land bordering Canada, to the Aleutian Island chain, extending 1000 miles southwest and separating the Bering Sea and the Pacific Ocean, Alaska's southern coast features a diversity of climates and communities. The mild and moist weather of Alaska's Southeast nurtures rainforests and agricultural valleys. Russian settlements, distinguished by the inhabitants' colorful dress and by the unique architecture of the Russian orthodox churches, are scattered throughout the southcentral and southeastern coastline. The quaint Norwegian fishing village of Petersburg in the Panhandle finds its antithesis in the military outposts on the blustery Aleutians. As the superb fishing of the Southeast features rockfish, salmon, red snapper and Pacific halibut, the scenic Kenai Peninsula southwest of Anchorage offers some of the best trout fishing, along with Arctic grayling, Dolly Varden and northern pike. Kodiak Island, south of the Kenai Peninsula, is a center for king crab fishing and processing.

More remote and colder than the southeast, Alaska's western coast is a place where time has stood relatively still. Eskimo villages and fishing outposts are separated from one another by vast tracts of wilderness. Westward, into the Bering Sea, Alaska's Pribilof Islands remain the primary breeding grounds for the fur seal. These sea mammals flock to the island in May, when the barking of the teeming herds can be heard from miles away. Over 180 species of birds, some very rare, can be seen on the Pribilofs, one of the largest bird sanctuaries in the world.

In the Far North the Arctic slope gives way to a twisting coastline hemmed in by ice much of the year. On Alaska's northernmost point, Barrow does not see the sun rise above the horizon for three months in midwinter. Along much of the remote northern coastline, buildings are constructed from driftwood and salvage. Alaska's northern shore runs eastward into the Yukon, where the Beaufort Sea comprises the northern boundary of Canada's most western region.

Surrounded by the Pacific and Arctic Oceans and the Bering and Chukchi Seas, Alaska is distinguished by the size and diversity of its coastline. Hundreds of islands, many unsettled, feature virgin forests and natural harbors. Cruise ships, one of Alaska's most popular forms of exploration, glide through the Panhandle's Inside Passage and through steep fjords. In the North, Eskimos hunt whales and seals in walrus-skin boats powered by outboard motors, signifying the marriage of past and present, and oil is extracted and transported through an artery that supplies the lifeblood for Alaska's emerging economy.

15 Icebergs from Portage Glacier drift in Portage Lake on the northeast side of Alaska's Kenai Peninsula.

16/17 A crab boat plies the waters near Kodiak, off Alaska's Kodiak Island south of the Kenai Peninsula.

18 Fish and salmon eggs dry over timber in Kotzebue, an Eskimo village on Alaska's Baldwin Peninsula above the Arctic Circle.

19 Halibut on display advertises fishing charters in Homer, on the southwestern coast of the Kenai Peninsula.

20 A fishing boat motors out of Kachemak Bay near Homer in the early morning darkness.

21 A slickered fisherman measures an Alaskan king crab.

22/23 Kayaking in Alaska's southeastern Glacier Bay in the light of the midnight sun.

24 A group of walruses basks on the rocks on Round Island, part of Walrus Islands State Game Sanctuary in southwestern Alaska's Bristol Bay.

25 Bull walruses congregate on Round Island's West Beach, below North Point, in midsummer.

26/27 A unique breed of sunbathers enjoys Saint Paul's beach in the Pribilof Islands.

28 Colorful tufted puffins perch on a cliff on Saint
Paul Island. The Pribilofs harbor almost 200
varieties of birds.

29 A northern fur seal rookery in the Pribilofs,
where thousands of seals gather to breed in May.

30 top Tiny wooded islands are found in Sitka Sound, part of Alaska's southeastern Panhandle region.

30 bottom A bush pilot makes a mail delivery by seaplane at Olga Bay on Kodiak Island.

31 The sun sets over a salt lagoon on Saint Paul Island.

32 Ancient Margerie Glacier dwarfs a cruise ship in Glacier Bay's Tarr Inlet.

33 Shimmering light from the setting sun breaks through the clouds as a cruise ship makes its way through Glacier Bay.

34/35 The icy wilderness at Glacier Bay was called 'Thunder Bay' by the Indians because of the loud crashes caused by icebergs breaking off, or calving, into the water.

36 *Through a rock formation at Kenai Fjords National Park, the Kenai Mountains can be glimpsed rising abruptly from the sea.*

37 *A stranded iceberg striated with debris floats in the waters of the Gulf of Alaska.*

CITIES AND TOWNS

The cities and towns of Alaska and the Yukon are characterized by a wealth of robust, exhilarating and even peculiar celebrations. From Cordova's Iceworm Festival to Anchorage's Fur Rendezvous, and from Petersburg's Little Norway Festival to Whitehorse's Yukon Sourdough Rendezvous, the range of events tell a little bit about the region's history and the character of its inhabitants. Dogsled races, sportscar races on ice, rafting races, contests for the longest beard, baseball games on snowshoes, native dancing and drama, and rodeo events point to both the humor and the spirit of adventure that seems so prevalent in the people of Alaska and the Yukon.

Many cities and towns of this vast land originated with the chaotic influx of goldseekers in the late 1800s. The Yukon's Dawson City, once gateway to the gold fields, supported a population of about 31,000 at the turn of the century. Formerly capital of the Yukon, the city now harbors less than 1000 people, but keeps alive the spirit of its history in its architecture, taverns and festivals. The city also preserves the residences of Robert W Service and Jack London, whose writings immortalized an era in Yukon history. Whitehorse, the Yukon's seat of government since 1953, sprawls over 162 square miles and comprises the territory's only town with more than 1000 people. Dogs, sleds and mushers fly from all over Alaska and the Yukon to test their skill and endurance in Whitehorse's annual Rendezvous Dogsled Races in February. Established in 1900 with the completion of the White Pass and Yukon Route, the city today is the territorial headquarters for the Royal Canadian Mounted Police, and boasts about 15,000 inhabitants.

The capital of Alaska since 1906, Juneau has also been called the longest city in the world. Built on a ledge of land between Mount Juneau and the Gastineau Channel, Juneau stretches along the shore for 40 miles. Established soon after the discovery of gold there in 1880, Juneau today harbors an intriguing combination of museums and government buildings. Isolated by mountains, ice fields and water, this city of 20,000 is accessible only by sea and air. Juneau is not Alaska's largest city, however — that distinction belongs to Anchorage, located on Alaska's southern shore midway between Juneau and the Bering Sea. Surrounded by mountains and situated on Cook Inlet, Anchorage is an emerging world city. Its international airport sees more than three million travellers pass through annually. With a population of about 202,000, Anchorage has had phenomenal growth since its beginnings as a railroad construction base in 1917. The city's scenic location and many amenities make it popular with visitors and Alaskans alike.

North into Alaska's interior, Fairbanks is Alaska's largest non-coastal city. Fairbanks began in earnest in 1902 with the discovery of gold on the bank of the Chena River. Today the city hosts a variety of cultural events and sports; in addition, the University of Alaska, the airport, the terminus of the Alaska Highway, the proximity to a segment of the Alaska pipeline and the connection to Seward by railroad have all played their part in making Fairbanks Alaska's second largest city. In July, one of the features of the city's Golden Days celebration, commemorating the discovery of gold, is the World Eskimo, Indian and Aleut Olympics. Such contests of skill and strength as the high kick, knuckle hop, ear pull and seal-skinning are featured, and humor is added with the *muktuk* (whale blubber) eating contest.

Whether isolated in the wilderness or interconnected by roads and rails, whether crowded with gleaming skyscrapers or bisected by a dirt road lined with makeshift cabins, Alaska and the Yukon's cities and town are uniquely adapted to their surroundings. Inhabited by the diverse peoples who impart character and color to each settlement, these cities and towns are united by the common thread of a heritage that comes from living close to the land.

39 Kites dive and soar in the sky over Anchorage during Kite Day.

40/41 The Anchorage skyline glows with the light of sunset in August, viewed from Earthquake Park.

42 The lights of Anchorage reflect in the snow at night. Situated on the Gulf Coast, the city is Alaska's center for business and finance.

43 Anchored near Juneau, a cruise ship casts its festive reflection on the waters of Gastineau Channel.

44/45 Gastineau Peak provides a backdrop to the Juneau skyline and Harris Harbor at sunset.

46 Old, corrugated-tin roofed buildings are reflected in the water at Petersburg, a Norwegian
fishing town on Kupreanof Island in Alaska's
Panhandle.

47 The architecture of the rebuilt Saint Michael's
Cathedral in Sitka, with its Byzantine dome and
delicate spire, is characteristically Russian
Orthodox.

48 A view along the three-mile boardwalk of
Alaska's Panhandle town of Ketchikan, on the
island of Revillagigedo.

49 A house outside of Dawson City catches the
dramatic light before a squall.

50 A sunset view of Fairbanks, Alaska's second largest city, in early winter.

51 A blanket toss in Barrow, Alaska's northernmost city, on the Arctic Ocean. The blanket toss was once used by Eskimo hunters as a way to spot game.

52 A view of Juneau from Douglas Island shows the city nestled at the foot of Mount Juneau.

53 Summer twilight on Juneau's Franklin Street. Originally a gold mining settlement, Juneau stretches along a narrow shelf between Mount Juneau and the Gastineau Channel.

54/55 The pioneer spirit is alive in Skagway, a former goldrush outpost of Alaska's southeast, where the false-front buildings and dirt streets are unchanged.

56 A man motors through the dirt streets of Nome. Destroyed by fire and flood more than once, Nome's somewhat ramshackle appearance is heightened when houses are jacked up to compensate for permafrost heaves.

57 A working gold dredge outside of Nome. Established as a gold rush town at the turn of the century, Nome has a current population of 2500, down from its boom population of 40,000.

58/59 Homer Spit reaches into Kachemak Bay off southwestern Alaska's Kenai Peninsula.

60/61 Men fish off the dock in King Cove on the Alaska Peninsula.

62 The cluttered and inviting interior of a leather shop in Talkeetna, Alaska.

63 A king crab processing plant in Kodiak, where the King Crab Festival takes place in May.

64 Details of a totem in Ketchikan. Usually carved of cedar and painted red, blue and black, totem poles were created by Indians to mock an enemy, commemorate an event or tell a story.

65 An artisan in Nome displays ivory carvings, many of them based on native designs.

66 *A beached boat near Kluane Lake, at Destruction Bay in the Yukon.*

67 An abandoned silver mine in the Yukon's Silver City is a relic of Canadian history. Gold and silver enticed prospectors and settlers into the Yukon at the turn of the century.

MOUNTAINS AND COUNTRYSIDE

A land of snow, ice and frost, of glaciers and volcanoes, of dense forests and grassy plains, tundra and towering mountains, farms and broad river valleys, Alaska and the Yukon offer a rich diversity of landscapes. Mighty rivers roar with rushing water at spring break-up, and giant mountain ranges culminate in Mount McKinley, largest in the United States, and Mount Logan, largest in Canada. National parks and preserves spread across this vast land, protecting habitats of flora and fauna and providing wilderness retreats for hardy adventurers.

Alaska's Katmai National Park and Preserve encompasses 4000 square miles of the northern Alaska Peninsula. Established in 1918, the park features ocean fjords, volcanic lakes, glaciers, mountains, forests and the Valley of Ten Thousand Smokes. The site of violent volcanic and earthquake action in 1912, the Valley of Ten Thousand Smokes, once a verdant valley, is now an eerily beautiful and desolate wasteland. Alaska's best-known park is, of course, Denali National Park. Located in the state's interior and featuring Mount McKinley, the largest in all of North America, the park is accessible by train and harbors a variety of wildlife both large and small. The Yukon's Kluane National Park in the Southwest typifies the region's beauty — its sparkling lakes, lofty mountains, forested plains and wide valleys comprising a naturalists' paradise. Over 35 miles long, Kluane Lake is the Yukon's largest. Summer trout fishing yields some specimens 50 pounds.

The beauty of the land and its native wildlife is appreciated by those who seek it. Here, also, the land yields subsistence to others. Many Alaskans hunt to provide or to supplement the family diet. Original homesteaders can still be found, those who earned their property by building a cabin and living off the land. Forests and lakes yield lumber and fish for commercial and private use, and the land provides ample opportunities for skiing, hiking, climbing, snowmobiling, river-rafting, camping and bird-watching. With most of the population of Alaska and the Yukon residing in urban areas, the vast wilderness is sparsely populated, for it contains forested ravines and trickling creeks that no man has ever seen.

The contours of this great land are formed by the mountainous arc of the Alaska Range, extending 500 miles in southeast and southcentral Alaska, and the Brooks Range, extending from western Alaska to the Yukon in the North, and by the Coast Mountains of the southeastern Yukon and the many other mountain ranges of the Yukon. Vast treeless stretches of tundra, dotted with grazing caribou and carpeted by the delicate plants that live in a precarious balance within a harsh climate, comprise much of the lowland areas. Fertile valleys occupied by farms and winding rivers making their way from one settlement to another enrich a land that is at once barren and lush, flat and alpestrine. The heart of Alaska and the Yukon is found in its mountains and countryside.

69 Fireweed brightens the foothills in Alaska's Chugach State Park.

70/71 Light glows on the snow-capped mountains north of Fairbanks.

72 Sunset on the Yukon River, which flows for 2081 miles from above Whitehorse to the Bering Sea.

73 Alaska's Wrangell Mountains form a snowy backdrop to Silver Lake near Chitina.

74 A car pauses as caribou cross Glen Highway near Alaska's Tahneta Pass.

75 Part of the Alaska Highway winds through the wilderness between the Yukon's Whitehorse and Haines Junction. The 1520-mile-long highway ends at Fairbanks.

76 A dairy farm near Palmer in Alaska's fertile Matanuska Valley northeast of Anchorage. The valley, which was settled by drought-stricken Midwest farmers in 1935, now produces half the state's crops.

77 A church and outbuildings in Circle, by the Yukon River northeast of Fairbanks. This town is the northernmost point on the continent's inter-connecting highway system.

78 Colorfully-dressed Russian children play on a slide in a Russian village near Anchor Point on Alaska's Kenai Peninsula.

79 A barefooted Russian woman tills the soil in her garden near Anchor Point. Attracted by fur trade, Russians colonized Alaska beginning in the eighteenth century.

80/81 The reflections of mountain and cloud are fragmented by hundreds of lilypads in this still Alaskan lake near Seward.

82 A log cabin on the Yukon's Tagish Lake is dwarfed by the embankment. The spidery arms of this lake dip south into British Columbia.

83 The trans-Alaska pipeline, carrying one and a half million barrels of oil a day from the Arctic shore to Valdez on the Gulf of Alaska, winds through the countryside near Fairbanks.

84 *Fall foliage shimmers against a gray sky along the Alaska Highway near Tok.*

85 *The feathery heads of cotton grass color a meadow by Lake Louise, northeast of Anchorage.*

86 A trapper cabin, stocked with firewood, near Dezedeasch Lake in the southern Yukon.

87 A modern-day prospector, who works the Kantishna Hills placer mine, poses for the camera.

88/89 An Alaskan brown bear sow with three cubs fishes in the Brooks River in Katmai National Park and Preserve.

90 A river cuts through volcanic silt in southwestern Alaska's Katmai National Park. Devastated in 1912 by volcanic eruptions and earthquakes, Katmai today harbors more than 30 species of land mammals.

91 The moon rises over volcanoes in Katmai National Park.

THE ARCTIC

The Arctic region of Alaska, stretching from the Yukon to the Chukchi Sea, comprises a third of the state. A land extreme in its climate and topography, and untamed, the Arctic reveals Alaska's past more than does any other region. Eskimo settlements can be found in Kotzebue, on the western coast, along the Kobuk River which empties into the sea near Kotzebue, in Point Hope, on a spit of land that juts into the Chukchi Sea, and in many other villages of the Arctic. Old ways of life blend with new, as Eskimos clothe themselves in home-sewn fur jackets and mail-order items, stock their freezers with both whale meat and TV dinners, and use both dogsleds and snowmobiles for winter transportation. In most areas the traditional sod and driftwood dwellings have been replaced by prefabricated wooden houses.

The Far North can be reached only by air. Remote and treeless, the area is surprisingly populated, with about 18,000 residents. During the remarkably mild summer months hillsides are blanketed in wildflowers and children play in t-shirts. The jagged, treeless peaks of the Brooks Range stretch from eastern to western boundaries, isolating the broad shelf of the Arctic slope, which slants into the Arctic Ocean. On the Arctic's northermost point, Barrow has a population of about 3000, most of whom are Eskimo. Only 1200 miles from the North Pole, Barrow exists in complete darkness for three months in midwinter, and in continual light for three months in midsummer. East of Barrow, Prudhoe Bay is the northern terminus of the trans-Alaska pipeline. Huge crews of workers labor to bring oil from below the 2000-foot permafrost. Supplies are received by boat from the East, and equipment is moved by huge trucks whose doughnut tires are so wide that they do no damage to the fragile plants of the tundra. The term 'tundra,' from the Russian word meaning 'where the trees are not,' takes on new meaning here.

Harsh but not barren, the Arctic land and its waters harbor a range of wildlife, from walrus and seals to polar bears and foxes, caribou, mountain sheep and whales. Gates of the Arctic National Park and Preserve, on the North Slope of the Brooks Range, encompasses more than eight million acres in northcentral Alaska. One of the finest wilderness areas in the world, the park is covered with shrubs and tundra. Caribou roam freely across the North Slope tundra, their summer feeding grounds.

The unique spectacles of the midnight sun and the aurora borealis, or northern lights, lend an almost mystical or primeval air to this primitive land. Here, past and present meld in a region that has both Eskimo settlements and all the modern technology of oil extraction at Prudhoe Bay. Tundra and mountains, ice fields and wildflowers coexist in a land unlike any other.

93 A partially frozen river winds through the snowy forests of the Brooks Range.

94/95 Eskimos in Kotzebue take in their fishing boat. Located on the Baldwin Peninsula north of the Arctic Circle, Kotzebue is about 80 percent Eskimo.

96 An arctic loon nests in the reeds on a lake
shore in the north country.

97 A float plane flies past the Arrigetch Peaks of
the Brooks Range in Alaska's Gates of the Arctic
National Park and Preserve.

*98 An old wooden cabin nestles in the snow in
Arctic Village in the foothills of the Brooks Range.*

99 An optimistic sign in Barrow, 'the crossroads of the Arctic.'

100 An Athabascan Indian child peers around the corner of a log cabin in Chalkyitsik, just north of the Arctic Circle in northeastern Alaska.

101 top Dressed in a flowered parka and variations of the traditional mukluks, or fur boots, an Eskimo woman in the Kobuk area holds strips of dried caribou.

101 bottom Many Eskimos are excellent storytellers, as is this friendly woman in the Kobuk area. The scenic Kobuk River country contains several Eskimo villages and Kobuk Valley National Park.

102/103 The midnight sun casts its strange light on the Arctic Ocean at Barrow.

104/105 A moored motorboat is silhouetted against the dramatic sky of the midnight sun at Kotzebue.

DENALI NATIONAL PARK

Denali National Park and Preserve has, as its outstanding feature, the largest mountain in North America, Mount McKinley. At 20,230 feet, this towering mountain can be seen all the way from Anchorage, 237 miles away, on a clear day. Named for President William McKinley by prospector William A Dickey in 1896, the mountain's official name is Denali, the Athabascan word meaning 'The High One.' McKinley's highest, southern summit was first scaled in 1913, and since that time numerous expeditions have achieved this glorious feat.

Located north of Anchorage and south of Fairbanks, the six million acre park straddles the lofty Alaska Range. Denali National Park was established in 1917 and expanded by 6094 square miles in 1978 to include all of Mount McKinley and the Cathedral Spires. Accessible by railroad and by road, the park preserves the ecosystems of tundra and mountains, forests and lakes. With a scant 14 miles of park road open to private vehicles, care is taken that visitors do not disturb the copious wildlife. Lichens, wildflowers — including the brilliant fireweed and delicate lupines — mosses and small shrubs flourish on the tundra, which blazes into color in late August. This season is also the time to admire Denali's forests, where spruce, poplar, aspen, birch and willow create a mosaic of color over the foothills. In winter the park is patrolled by rangers on dogsled, a means of transport and recreation also available to the hardy adventurer, along with cross-country skiing and mountaineering.

Denali offers Alaska's best opportunities to view wildlife in its native habitat. Dall sheep dot the hillsides and cliffs, grizzly bears wander the forests and meadows, caribou gather in June before their northern migration in July, lakes are filled with beavers and nesting waterfowl, moose sip icy water from mountain streams, and the fields and woods offer food and shelter to the Canada lynx, porcupine, fox, wolf, snowshoe hare, squirrel, marmot, black bear and coyote. Almost 40 species of mammals are found here, as well as 130 varieties of birds — from the migratory Arctic warbler and golden plover to the resident golden eagle, great horned owl and ptarmigan, Alaska's state bird.

Canoeing, berry picking, fishing, mountain climbing, hiking, kayaking, bird watching and photographing are some of the pleasures available in this beautiful wilderness park. The many sights of Denali National Park include the mighty Muldrow Glacier, which flows northward from the Alaska Range, lofty Mount McKinley serenely reflected in Wonder Lake, a trumpeter swan gliding across a still pond, an eagle soaring over forested peaks, a curious ermine scampering over the snow, and a sunset sky coloring snowy hillsides in violet and gold.

107 Mount Deborah looms in the background of this view of Denali's Nenena River Valley.

108/109 Part of the Alaska Range, culminating in 20,230-foot-high Mount McKinley, is reflected in Wonder Lake.

110/111 Mount McKinley is located in the six-million acre Denali National Park. The mountain's official name is 'Denali' as well, which derives from the Athabascan Indian word meaning 'The High One.'

112 A massive caribou bull picks his way through
the underbrush.

113 *King of the northern woods, a grizzly bear surveys its domain.*

114/115 *A moose cow and her calf wade in a mountain pond.*

116 An adult porcupine peers at the camera. Reserved as a wilderness area in 1917, Denali harbors a wealth of wildlife by preserving their native habitats.

117 A wily ermine is poised by a stump. Almost 40 species of land mammals live in Denali National Park.

118/119 Dall rams lounge on a mountainside. Their cloven hooves aid their footing in the mountainous terrain and enable them to dig through the snow to reach edible plants.

120 *Two weeks out of the nest, a young hawk owl perches on a dead limb.*

121 *Glazed with winter's first snow, evergreens rim a remote pond in Denali's wilderness.*

122/123 *Sunset illuminates the crags and folds of the Alaska Range.*

124 A dogsled driver fastens down the sled as dogs peer out of their travel compartments.

125 A dogsled team stops for a breather on a path through Denali National Park.

126/127 Day hikers in the Kantishna hills survey the grand spectacle of Denali National Park.